HOW TO WRITE A BOOK PROPOSAL THAT SELLS!

15 Secrets to Earning Six Figures for Your Book

DAWNA STONE

BAY POINT
media

Printed in the United States of America

First Edition: June 2017
10 9 8 7 6 5 4 3 2 1

ISBN 978-0-9992123-2-5

Edited by Corinne Whiting
Cover design and formatting by **Archangel Ink**

Disclaimer: This book provides advice but does not guarantee any specific outcomes or results.

Trademarked names are used throughout the book. Instead of placing a trademark symbol after every occurrence of a trademarked name, we use names in an editorial fashion only, with no intention of infringement of the trademark. Where such designations appear in the book, they have been printed with initial caps.

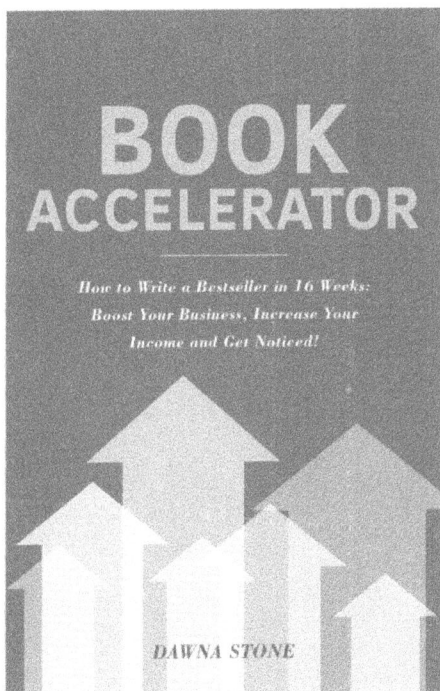

Contents

Introduction

Although self-publishing has become more mainstream and many extremely successful authors have emerged through the process, publishing with a large publisher still provides a certain level of clout. And although media outlets are rapidly changing and increasingly putting self-published authors on air, some big national shows continue to steer clear of self-published book authors (unless they already have gained overwhelming notoriety).

How to Write a Book Proposal That Sells! provides the tools you need to develop a book proposal that sets you apart from all the other authors and makes your book worthy of a six-figure deal.

Writing a great book proposal and landing a publishing deal will bring the added benefit of setting a hard deadline for your completed manuscript. I know from experience that finding time to write a book can be difficult, especially if you're not a full-time writer. In fact, it took me nearly two decades to finish writing the first book I started (but more on that later).

To date, I've written four books—three with large publishers and one self-published. I wrote my first one, a 60,000-word book, in less than 12 weeks, my second and third books, both consisting of 40,000-plus words, in under 10 weeks and my fourth book, 30,000 words, in less than six weeks!

I received a five-figure book deal for my first book, I self-published my second book, and I received a six-figure deal for my third book. Both advances came from large, well-known publishing houses. My fourth book was published in partnership with "Shape" magazine.

I share these successes because, prior to getting my first book deal, I spent nearly 20 years trying to complete a book. I would start writing and maintain the momentum for a few days, only to get distracted and eventually push the project aside. It wasn't that I wasn't motivated or passionate about getting my book done; I just never seemed to find the time to make my writing a priority. There always seemed to be something else taking center stage, so the book writing got shoved to the sidelines.

I didn't finally complete my first book because I suddenly found extra time; it happened because I received a book deal. An agent convinced me to write a book proposal and to "shop it around" to assess interest. When Hachette Book Group (HBG), one of the "big five" publishing companies along with Holtzbrinck/Macmillian, Penguin Random House, HarperCollins and Simon & Schuster, gave me a five-figure book deal, I no longer had any excuses for procrastinating. In fact, delaying the work was no longer an option; I had a strict deadline I must adhere to. This accountability helped (or I should say forced) me to make my book writing a priority and to set a mandatory writing schedule, in order to meet my deadlines.

It all started with a book proposal, which turned into a book deal and eventually evolved into a completed book— one that quickly hit the bestseller list! Of course producing a strong book proposal is no small task, but it is much easier and less time-consuming than writing an entire book. And with the right framework, the process becomes much more manageable. A book proposal also forces you to spend sufficient time developing your concept, audience and voice, and it helps you better understand your market and competition. These are all steps that cumulatively help you write a bestseller when the time comes to start your book.

To date, I have written three book proposals, all of which sold. As mentioned above, one sold to HBG, one to Rodale Inc. (the publisher of well-known books like "The South Beach Diet," "The Atkins Diet" and "Wheat Belly" as well as popular magazines like "Women's Health," "Men's Health" and "Prevention"). The other sold to Meredith Corporation, which owns a vast number of popular magazines including "Better Homes and Gardens," "Shape," "Allrecipes," "Parents" and "EatingWell."

Both large publishing houses revealed that my book proposal immediately captured their attention. One of my editors even declared it one of the best she had ever seen. So what makes a book proposal worthy of a five- or six-figure deal? A strong book proposal will have the following 15 characteristics.

An exceptional proposal:

1) Has a strong title page
2) Is clear, concise and consistent
3) Includes a summary
4) Contains a high-level outline or table of contents
5) Includes an author bio
6) Shares your platform
7) Includes a detailed marketing plan
8) States how you will invest both your time and money
9) Includes one or two sample chapters
10) Describes your target audience
11) Includes a competitive analysis

12) Has been edited with as much care as your book

13) Exhibits both style AND substance

14) Shows the potential for a series, if possible

15) Includes testimonials, praise and endorsements when possible

How to Write a Book Proposal That Sells! provides the tools you need to develop a book proposal that sets you apart from all the other authors and makes your book worthy of a six-figure deal. Use the step-by-step framework to create a book proposal that sells!

Chapter 1:
Title Page

Make sure your proposal has a strong title page. Typically the title page only contains your book title (including subtitle), your name, the copyright symbol and year. You can also include contact information on this page, or leave that for the proposal's final page.

You may wonder how a page that typically features only 10 to 20 words can make a statement. It can! This page will be the first thing the publisher sees before reviewing your proposal. Make sure you've invested the time and effort to come up with a great book title and subtitle. In my book, *Book Accelerator—How to Write a Bestseller in 16 Weeks: Boost Your Business, Increase Your income and Get Noticed!* I dedicate an entire chapter to developing a title that sells!

The title is one of your most important tools when it comes to selling books, and the same rings true when trying to "sell" your idea to a publisher.

I realize the title you use in your proposal may not end up on the cover of your future book, but you should still give it the time and effort it deserves.

A title that captivates the publisher will be:

- Interesting—piques the reader's interest
- Informative—explains what the book is about
- To-The-Point—uses words or sentences that are not too lengthy
- Marketable—states what the book will do for the reader
- Discoverable—uses keywords that are easily searchable

Take the time necessary to come up with a title that adheres to these five rules, and your proposal will be off to a promising start.

Although not necessary, if you happen to have a professionally-developed sample cover, include it on your title page. However, if the cover has not been designed by a professional, you're better off simply going with text and no artwork. I've done both. I believe that, if done correctly, the cover design can help set your proposal apart from others.

Book Proposal

For

The Healthy You Diet

The 14-Day Plan for Weight Loss with 100 Delicious

Recipes for Clean Eating

By Dawna Stone

(Text Only)

Proposal for

Junk Food Funk

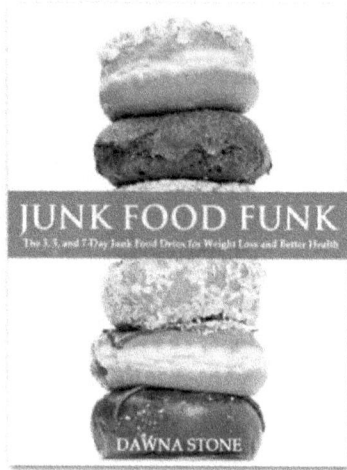

By Dawna Stone

(Sample Cover)

Although some of my cover samples have been very similar in design to the final version, all have been somewhat altered throughout the process.

On the left, find the sample cover that I included on the title page of my book proposal; on the right, see the actual cover that the publisher designed.

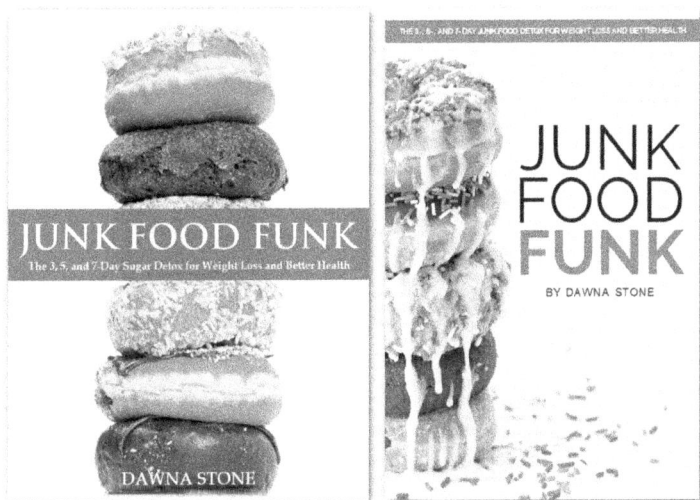

It's up to you whether or not you include a sample cover, but always take the time to create a book title that will build interest and compel the publisher to continue turning pages.

Chapter 2:
Clear, Concise and Consistent

Make sure your proposal is clear, concise and consistent. I focus a great deal on this topic in my latest book, "Book Accelerator." Most people have no problem understanding the importance of maintaining clear, concise and consistent writing throughout their book, but they often don't carry that same level of attention to the book proposal.

Your book proposal should be no less important than your book, and your ability to "sell" your idea to a traditional publisher can hinge upon this fact. Book publishers look for your book proposal to be just as polished as your finished work. In fact, they will consider your proposal a direct reflection of your future book. A shoddy proposal will convince them that your book might also be inferior. But a well-written—clear, concise and consistent—proposal will give the publisher confidence in your abilities to deliver a book of the same caliber.

Focus on creating an exceptional proposal that highlights your absolute best work throughout. If you provide one or two sample chapters, make sure you're showcasing your strongest examples. The book proposal isn't a place to hold back your talents; it's your chance to show it off!

Chapter 3:
Summary

Make sure your proposal contains a detailed overview of the book that will capture the publisher's interest. I like to include a brief description of every book section. I use the rule from chapter two and keep my overview clear, concise and consistent. A strong overview will keep the publisher hooked, but a weak one may mean they read no further.

Make sure your summary includes all the most important elements in the book proposal. When writing the summary, I always ask myself this one question: "If the publisher reads nothing but the summary, will they have received the most important information?"

In the summary, I include a brief overview of the book, the most impressive parts of my author bio and platform and other pertinent data that I want to highlight from the overall proposal. Basically, this is your book's sales sheet, containing all the most important items to captivate the publisher and make him or her want to offer you a book deal.

I tend to use a very similar structure for my summary, no matter the book genre. The structure I follow is:

- A short paragraph that describes the book and states why it's needed

- A brief author bio that simply highlights the most important points

- The key components of my author platform that will help me reach the target audience

- A paragraph that explains why I'm uniquely qualified to write the book

- A paragraph that states my commitment to the project and how I can help sell copies

If you have any unique attributes that set you apart from other authors, make sure you include those in the summary. You can provide further details in one of the main sections of the proposal, but make sure you also highlight them in your overview. This can include anything from your understanding of the market to direct access to a specific demographic or any other interesting facts that could help sell more copies of the book.

For example, I had a well-known (in the book publishing world) social media consultant lined up to work with me should I get a book deal. My proposal mentioned that I would use part of my advance to hire this individual to help me promote the book during its launch. Although this wasn't necessary, it was no doubt a unique proposition that showed how committed I felt to making the book a success—something that very well might have set my proposal apart from the dozens the publishing house receives on a daily basis.

You don't have to hire a social media expert (or any expert, for that matter), but if you have a unique way to market your book, include that idea in the proposal. Anything that shows your commitment to the book's success will help you stand out in a large crowd of other authors vying for a book deal. Touching on this in your overview will ensure that the publisher understands the scope of your brilliant ideas, even if they don't proceed to read your entire proposal.

Chapter 4:
High-Level Outline

Make sure your proposal contains a high-level outline or table of contents (TOC). I always include a full TOC with my proposal. This gives the publisher a better feel for the book's layout, as well as what you're promising to deliver with the finished manuscript.

Remember, the TOC can always change. Just because you include it in your proposal doesn't mean anything is set in stone. In fact, each of the table of contents included in my proposals got altered in some way for the final version of the book—some with minor changes and others with substantial changes.

In my books, I typically aim to have three to six sections and 12 to 15 chapters. This, however, is merely a benchmark that helps me during the planning process. As I build out the TOC, it often evolves into an altered structure that works best with each specific book topic.

My first book had only two sections and 15 chapters. My second had four sections and 19 chapters, my third had three sections and 16 chapters, my fourth had 7 sections and 24 chapters, and my most recent work "Book Accelerator" featured nine sections and 22 chapters.

No matter how many sections or chapters you include, make sure your TOC flows naturally and that the chapter sequence makes sense to the reader. Also, pay attention to the section and chapter headings. You may not need to spend as much time and effort on this wording as you do with your book title (but don't discount the headers' importance either).

Since the publisher initially gets only a glimpse of your book, the TOC needs to be as strong as possible to pique his or her interest and to generate excitement.

If you plan to also include acknowledgements, a foreword, an introduction or any appendixes in your book, include these in your TOC as well.

A strong TOC can mark the difference between getting rejected and getting the deal!

On the following page you'll find examples of three tables of contents from my previous books:

Book Accelerator

How to Write a Bestseller in 16 Weeks: Boost Your Business, Increase Your Income, and Get Noticed!

Table of Contents

JUNK FOOD FUNK

The 3-, 5- and 7-Day Junk Food Detox for Weight Loss

Table of Contents

LETTER FROM THE AUTHOR

The Healthy You Diet

The 14-Day Plan for Weight Loss with 100 Delicious Recipes for Clean Eating

Table of Contents

As you can see, all three tables of contents look very different in terms of section and chapter amounts. But each TOC provides the publisher with a solid idea of the structure and content the book provides. Always provide the book's TOC in your proposal.

Chapter 5:
Author Bio

Make sure your proposal states why you are qualified to write the book. I always include an author bio in my proposal, along with specifics on what makes me a subject matter expert. This can include past experience, credentials, etc.

It can be uncomfortable to speak highly about oneself, but your author bio is the one place you really need to toot your own horn. This is your chance to make the publisher think, "Wow, I really want to work with this person."

Make sure you tailor you bio to your book's topic. For example, the publisher doesn't need to know you worked for two years in the fast food industry if you're writing a book titled "Dog Training Made Easy." It might be pertinent information, however, if the title of your book is "Getting Ahead in Business: From Fast Food to the Boardroom." Keep past experience relevant.

If you have an interesting fact that could set you apart from other authors and help you sell more books and grow a bigger following, include that fact in this section. Also include clubs, associations and other notable mentions, if these will help you promote your book.

If you have had prior success authoring other books (self-published or traditionally- published), share those details here as well.

If you're still struggling to write your bio, try looking at other authors' bios for inspiration. You can find bios on most authors' websites or within the covers of their books.

At any moment, I have several different bios written and ready to go. I have both short and long versions for speaking engagements and a detailed bio for book proposals. I also have two separate bios—one for my health and wellness readers and one for my business audience.

Below find a sample of my speaker's bio as well as a bio from my most recent book proposal (a health and wellness book).

Speaker's Bio

Dawna Stone is a business owner, author and health and wellness expert. She is the founder of the St. Pete Wine & Food Festival and President and Publisher of "LocalsDISH" magazine.

Dawna writes for numerous popular magazines and websites and was named one of the best clean-eating bloggers by "Prevention" magazine. Her cookbook, "The Healthy You Diet!" has been one of Amazon's best sellers. Her newest book "Junk Food Funk" was published in partnership with "Shape" magazine.

Dawna is a mom of two young kids, which she considers her greatest accomplishment. She enjoys running, yoga and, of course, cooking.

Dawna's inspirational talks dive into her professional and personal experiences as a businesswoman, reality TV star, competitive athlete, best-selling author and mother of two. Dawna describes the fears she's overcome in building two multi-million dollar companies and how she's turned her failures into successes along the way.

Healthy You Diet Author Bio

Dawna Stone is an **author, entrepreneur, motivational speaker, self-made millionaire and health, fitness and wellness expert.** Through her new book, "Healthy You!: 14 Days to Quick and Permanent Weight Loss and a Healthier, Happier You," as well as frequent local and national television, radio and speaking appearances, Dawna serves as a role model and inspiration to men and women everywhere.

As the founder of "Women's Running" magazine and the Women's Half Marathon series, Dawna has helped thousands lead healthier lives. She has also served as a celebrity spokesperson for the American Heart Association's "Go Red for Women" campaign and contributed health and wellness articles to numerous newspapers and magazines.

In 2005, Dawna appeared on—and won—NBC's "The Apprentice: Martha Stewart." She spent the following year working closely with Stewart while developing a variety of projects for Martha Stewart Living Omnimedia, including a regular column in "Body+Soul" magazine (later renamed "Whole Living").

Dawna has appeared regularly on TV talk shows like "The Today Show," "MARTHA," and "Bethenny," as well as morning news programs on all four major networks— NBC, CBS, ABC and Fox. She also hosted her own show on Sirius Satellite Radio called "Health and Fitness Talk with Dawna Stone," as well as a regular television segment on Fox called "Healthy Living with Dawna Stone."

Her latest book, "Healthy You!," hit Amazon's bestseller list as soon as it was released and climbed as high as number 11 in the "Diet and Weight Loss" category, without any major publisher backing or promotions.

Prior to writing "Healthy You!" Dawna was a financial analyst for Wall Street investment bank Morgan Stanley, a consultant for Deloitte Consulting, President of PR*Nutrition, Senior VP of Operations at Active.com and Chief Marketing Officer for a $700 million-dollar publicly traded company. Dawna launched "Women's Running" magazine in 2004 and the Women's Half Marathon series in 2009 and sold both companies in 2012.

An American Council on Exercise (ACE)-certified health coach, Dawna earned her bachelor's degree from UC Berkeley and her masters degree from UCLA. An avid runner and Ironman triathlete, she lives in St. Petersburg, Florida, with her husband, 9-year-old daughter and 7-year-old son.

Remember, in addition to selling your book idea, you are also selling yourself. Don't hold back or be shy when it comes to promoting your talents and strengths. Some may have an idea convincing enough to immediately prompt a publisher to make a deal, but most of us need to leave an impression with our background and expertise.

Chapter 6:
Highlight Your Platform

Make sure your proposal highlights your platform. What is an author platform? Your platform is how you reach potential readers. Your platform can be made up of several different outlets such as social media, TV, radio, speaking engagements, blog traffic, etc. Your author bio and platform can overlap in some places, but they really serve two distinct purposes. As we discussed in the previous chapter, your author bio should help introduce you to the publisher—specifically clarifying who you are and why you are qualified to write the book. Your author platform should tell the publisher how you plan to reach your target audience, therefore explaining how you can help sell more books

The most common reason for rejection in the publishing world is a non-existent author platform. Fortunately, it is now easier to build a platform than ever before. Prior to social media, you had to get on TV or radio—or write for a popular newspaper or magazine—to garner an impressive following (or you had to have previously published a successful book). Today, almost anyone with an area of expertise can build a platform, as long as they are willing to invest the time and effort.

If you are able to reach and influence a large number of people in your target market, you can establish a significant platform that the publisher will find valuable.

In your proposal, state all the different areas that make up your author platform. A simple way to do this involves splitting your platform into online and offline reach. Below are some of the most common platform builders. Highlight the ones that might be part of your platform.

Online:

- Your personal blog
- Podcasts
- Online articles
- Videos/YouTube channel
- Email
- Newsletters
- Guest blogging
- Online courses

Off-Line:

- Television
- Radio
- Speaking engagements
- Leadership roles in clubs or associations
- Magazine articles
- Newspaper articles
- Published books

Remember, your platform should convince the publisher that you have the visibility and reach to help sell books!

If you don't have a robust platform, use this section to share with the publisher how you plan to grow your following. Let them know you are building out your audience, and share any successes or interesting stats that prove you're moving in the right direction. For example, if your Facebook fans grew 20% last month, let it be known. Show the publisher you've been expending the effort to build a strong platform.

Chapter 7:
Detailed Marketing Plan

Make **sure your proposal** includes a detailed marketing plan. Today, publishers (both big and small) expect you to do most of the heavy lifting when it comes to marketing your book. Gone are the days when you simply wrote a good book and left the rest to the experts; now you have to be a marketing expert, too! I have found that providing a draft of one's marketing plan in the proposal sets you apart and shows you are coming to the party with something to offer.

I typically include a one- to two-page plan that shares the different forms of marketing I will contribute to the book. This could include social media posts, email blasts, speaking opportunities, video marketing and partnership marketing. Any opportunity you have to get the word out about your book can become a marketing strategy that the publisher will value.

If you already have a strong following on any social media platform, restate it again here and share how you will utilize these fans to increase potential book sales. The publishers want to know that the author can drive sales as much, or even more, as they can. Also, if you have a large email database, focus on it. Email marketing is one of the best ways to reach potential book buyers; the stronger and more focused your list, the more value it carries.

Below is the marketing plan I included in my *Healthy You! Diet* cookbook proposal. Admittedly, this was a very robust plan. Yours doesn't need to be quite as complex, but use my plan as a framework, and be as detailed as you can. Your sample marketing plan should show the publisher that you're invested and determined to put in sufficient effort to help make the book a success.

Marketing Plan: Healthy You Diet

AUTHOR BLOG AND WEBSITE

Maintain an active, fresh website with constant updates. (Website should be updated daily or weekly.)

Website: Readers

1) Establish relationship with "Healthy You!" readers. Offer a forum so that readers can communicate with the author and get their questions answered.

2) Offer readers additional information outside of "Healthy You!":

   a) Additional bonus recipes

   b) Food images

   c) Specific ingredient information

   d) Photos of reader recipes

   e) Testimonials

   f) Blog posts

   g) Forums

   h) How-to videos

Website: Non-Readers

1) Offer enough information about the book for non-readers to be pulled in and ultimately buy the book.

Blog

1) Create at least 2-4 new blog entries per week.

2) Host 'guest blogs' from related professionals and readers.

3) Include lots of photos in each blog post to engage interest.

4) Topics can be centered around bonus recipes, nutritional information, new data and statistics related to healthy eating, the health food industry, documentaries, books/author interviews, healthy living articles, author experiences, etc.

   a) Reader should be able to link to other social media avenues as often as possible.

EMAIL MARKETING

Create email campaigns promoting the book and/or book signings to local and national distribution lists.

Distribution Lists:

1) Friends and family

2) Companies and organizations that we have worked with previously

Partnerships

1) Inclusion in partners' newsletters and email campaigns

SOCIAL NETWORKING AND SOCIAL MEDIA

Facebook

1) Connect with anyone interested in healthy cooking/ wholesome eating/weight loss.

2) Incorporate the following:

    a) Personal sharing (photos, updates, etc.)

    b) Photos!

    c) Recipes

    d) News articles

    e) Inspirational messages

    f) Questions

    g) Giveaways

3) Post 1 to 3 times per day.

4) Connect Facebook and Instagram to Twitter.

Instagram

1) Focus on food photos.

2) Photograph everything related to healthy eating and cooking.

3) 90% of all uploads should relate to healthy eating/cooking.

Twitter

1) Continue to build Twitter following.

    a) Provide informative content.

    b) Provide links to recipes and recent blog posts or articles.

2) Prior to the book's launch, follow a minimum of 25 new people a day (those related to cooking, healthy eating and weight loss).

Pinterest

1) Continue to build a presence on Pinterest—especially focusing on the most popular boards i.e. clean and healthy recipes.

2) Develop a new board for "Healthy You!"

LinkedIn

1) Continue to use LinkedIn as a tool to connect with industry leaders, TV producers, radio personalities, etc.

YouTube

1) Continue to expand YouTube presence by uploading 2-4 new videos a month.

OTHER BLOGS

1) Virtual book tours

2) Author interviews on top healthy eating, cooking or weight loss blogs

3) Book giveaways

4) Guest blogging

AUDIO AND VIDEO PROMOTIONS

1) Video introducing the book and premise for Amazon author page.

2) Host videos on website.

    a) Release 2-4 videos per month.

    b) Set schedule to shoot up to 10 (60- 90-second) videos.

        i)   Welcome/intro to "Healthy You!"

      ii) Prepare your pantry

      iii) How-to videos for each recipe

  c) Encourage readers to send in videos as they prepare the recipes.

3) YouTube Channel

  a) Continue to build YouTube following and post 2-4 new videos per month.

PROMOTIONAL GIVEAWAYS/CONTESTS

1) Launch promotional book giveaways via social media and popular blogs.

2) Host giveaways (promotional items, non-book related) on book's website/blog/social media to draw people into the page and add 'likes'.

ONLINE ADVERTISING

1) Target women interested in health, wellness, cooking, clean eating and weight loss.

  a) Facebook – daily ads following book release

Chapter 8:
Prove You're Invested
(The #1 Secret!)

Make sure your proposal states how you will invest both your time and money in promoting the book. I believe this is the number one thing that set me apart. You can no longer count on the publisher to do it all, and most pubs expect you to handle a lot of the marketing—or at least show that you're walking in from the get-go with desirable contributions.

In addition to sharing my marketing plan in my proposal, I always include a section stating my willingness to invest some of my own money in the marketing of the book. For example, in my cookbook proposal, I said I would invest $5,000 to $10,000 dollars of my own money to advertise the book on social media (Facebook ads, Google ads, etc.). Don't fret! This won't cost you a dime unless you get a book deal.

Investing your own money shows that you're committed to the project and willing to go the extra mile to make the book a success. If you express your commitment to the project, the publisher immediately realizes you are "all in" and ready to do anything necessary to help drive sales.

You may be thinking, I don't have $5k or $10k to spend on marketing. Remember, you only have to do this *if* you get the deal. Both my advances were large enough to easily use a portion of the advance to cover this additional expense.

You can always renegotiate these numbers once you land a deal, too. For example, you will have no trouble spending $10,000 on your book if you receive a $150,000 advance, right? If, however, you only received a $10,000 advance, you can go back to the publisher and explain that you can now only spend $2k of your own money (rather than the $5k to $10k mentioned in your proposal). In most cases, the publisher won't have an issue with this change.

You can also utilize your marketing budget to help negotiate a larger advance. If you receive an offer below what you had hoped for, you can negotiate a larger advance by stating that you will spend any additional dollars directly on marketing the book. As you can see, there are many options. For example, if you receive a $45,000 advance, you can try and negotiate a $50,000 or $60,000 advance by agreeing to use any additional dollars above the original

$45,000 on direct book advertising. Most publishers will be willing to negotiate.

Chapter 9:
Show Off Your Writing

Make sure your proposal includes at least one sample chapter from your book. This will allow the publisher to get a feel for your writing style. I have found that including two chapters is preferable, and I also always include the book's introduction.

Although including all three—two chapters and the introduction—may seem like overkill, I like that it allows me to showcase my writing and gives the publisher a feel for the book's voice and tone. The introduction also gives me the opportunity to further sell the concept to the publisher. To clarify, a good introduction is supposed to excite readers and make them feel good about their purchase. The book's introduction essentially acts as the book's promise to the reader and, if done well, can also make for a great sales tool when it comes to marketing your book idea to a potential publisher.

Below find the sample introductions from two of my recent books, "Book Accelerator" and the "Healthy You Diet." Read the introductions and —instead of reading them as a potential book buyer—imagine you are a publisher looking for a new book project. Notice how the introduction provides not only a nice overview, but also states what the book will deliver to the reader and why the author is qualified to provide that information.

Including a sample introduction in your book proposals allows you to restate all the most important aspects of your book one more time—and can ultimately help you secure a deal.

Sample Introduction: Book Accelerator

Publishing my first book changed my life for the better. It catapulted my income, opened countless doors and landed me five-figure speaking engagements and a six-figure traditional book deal, in addition to getting me regular appearances on TV and radio shows as an expert guest—ultimately providing me with even more credibility.

I believe that anyone who wants to write a book, feels passionate about a specific topic or has expertise worth sharing should publish; however, few ever get past the initial planning phase. My advice: Don't let another day go by while simply thinking about writing a book. Let "Book Accelerator" be your guide, with its proven step-by-step process that helps you go from the idea phase to completed book in as short a period as 16 weeks.

I wrote my first book—and all that has followed—by using the Book Accelerator methodology. I wrote each one while simultaneously running two companies and taking care of two young children. The Book Accelerator program provided me with a framework that kept me motivated and on track, and it will give you the tools needed to finish your book, too—no matter how busy you are or how many times you've tried before. If you're serious about writing a book and willing to give the process some time and effort, "Book Accelerator" is for you!

I know the Book Accelerator methodology works, because I've used it to write four bestsellers. Not only did each of my books hit Amazon's bestseller list, but they also helped me cumulatively earn hundreds of thousands of dollars.

Many dream of one day writing a book, but few ever follow through. I was almost one of those well-intentioned people. I had wanted to write a book for as long as I could remember. In fact, nearly 20 years went by from the day I wrote that first word to the moment the completed project finally got published. That first year, I even got so far as to create a title, subtitle, table of contents and several chapters; but that's where I stalled. About once a year, I would take out the book's rough start and vow to dig in again. But that enthusiasm would only last for a few days before the unfinished chapters would return to that dormant computer folder titled "My Book."

It wasn't until nearly two decades passed that I figured out a program that provided the structure and motivation needed to finally go all the way. As of today, I've used that same methodology to write a 60,000-word book in less than 16 weeks, both a 50,000- and 40,000-word book in under 12 weeks and a 30,000-word book in less than six!

I've also had very different experiences with each book. I've self-published, I've received five-figure and six-figure book deals (both from large publishing houses), and, for my most recent project, I've partnered with a popular national magazine. In fact, my self-published book did so well that a large publishing house ended up giving me a lucrative deal to expand on the original concept.

I'm sharing all of this because I used the Book Accelerator methodology to make every one of my books a success, and I am confident the program can help you do the same.

Book Accelerator will:

- Teach you how to write a best-selling book in less than 16 weeks, even if you currently don't know where to begin.

- Show you how to produce a high-quality, self-published book or how to get a traditional publisher to write you a five- or six-figure advance.

- Demonstrate how to use your book as a tool to boost your business or career, increase your income, gain new clients, customers or fans and become a sought-after expert in your field.

- Provide the strategies needed to build buzz for a book launch.

- Teach you how to monetize your book, earn passive income and get paid for your valuable knowledge.

- Help you build a platform for success!

A book can be the difference between simply doing well and becoming ultra successful. Don't wait another moment to get started. Let "Book Accelerator" help you become a best-selling author today!

Sample Introduction: Healthy You Diet

For the last decade I've shared my message of healthy eating and weight loss with millions. People often assume that I've always been slender and healthy, but trust me, that wasn't always the case. Just like so many others, I struggled with my weight and, as a result, with my health for many years.

When I graduated from college and moved to New York City to work as a financial analyst for a Wall Street investment bank, I started to pack on the pounds. It was bad enough that I had gained (and never lost) the ubiquitous freshman fifteen during my first year at school. Then, once I was out in the working world, it wasn't long before I added an additional 25 pounds to my frame—a total of 40 pounds!

For so long, I felt that I was the only person in the world who couldn't control her obsession with food. My life was consumed by food—what to eat and when to eat. Before one meal was finished, I was thinking about the next. Because my 14-hour days were so long, I rewarded myself by grabbing unhealthy foods and snacks at the company cafeteria. After a hard day at the office, it was reassuring to know that a box of cookies awaited me at home. Some people might have been happy with a couple of cookies, but I managed to eat the entire box in one sitting. If there were no goodies to look forward to at home, I stopped at the corner market for some frozen yogurt and a candy bar.

I knew my eating was out of control, but none of the diets I tried helped. And believe me, I tried them all— from well-known commercial weight loss programs to seeking assistance at a special weight loss clinic. At best, I'd lose a few pounds, but I'd always regain the weight (along with a bit extra).

Then one day, it dawned on me that the reason I couldn't lose weight and keep it off was because the diets and programs I used just weren't right for me! I hated getting publicly weighed in front of a roomful of strangers. I despised the tiny, tasteless pre-packaged meals. I didn't have time to make the complicated recipes I saw in magazines and books. I loathed the eating plan designed for me by a bodybuilder that consisted only of chicken, tuna and vegetables. I was miserable. And I was always craving more food, because nothing satisfied me. All of those diets proved useless for someone who loves food as much as me.

In order to find a weight loss program that worked and had everything I wanted—simple, yet delicious recipes, an occasional indulgence, dining out options—I had to create my own plan. Through trial and error, I finally discovered an eating plan that worked! The weight came off quickly and easily and, most importantly, it stayed off. I was no longer craving junk food between meals or desperately shoving unhealthy foods into my mouth.

Soon, colleagues, friends and family members noticed my weight loss and asked how I did it. It seemed that everyone was just as fed up and frustrated with traditional weight loss programs as I was. Although I never thought of what I consumed as "my plan," I was soon sharing my recipes and tips with anyone who asked, including local women's groups and clubs.

I spent the next six years working in the world of finance and strategy, with the exception of a two-year stint at graduate school. It became clear that my career in the financial world limited my ability to share with others what I discovered about eating well and losing weight. I decided to leave my job as a strategy consultant and accepted an offer to be president and general manager of a $20 million sports nutrition company. That job was my first official foray into a world that focused on health, wellness and fitness rather than investments, banking and management consulting.

In 2001, my husband and I moved to St. Petersburg, Florida, and I became the chief marketing officer for a $700 million publically traded company. Although it was a great company, I had become accustomed to working in an environment that inspired people to get healthy and live well. I missed helping others more than I realized. In 2003, I raised the money to launch a women's sports and fitness magazine—initially called "Her Sports" and later changed to "Women's Running"—which allowed me to share what I had learned about weight loss, nutrition and fitness with other busy women who felt as desperate as I had. As a result, I was asked to do a regular TV segment on Fox called "Healthy Living with Dawna Stone," allowing me to reach an even larger audience.

In 2006, I applied for and was selected as one of sixteen contestants on "The Apprentice: Martha Stewart." When I won the TV competition, hundreds of doors opened for me. I suddenly had my own weekly radio show. I wrote regular columns for "Body+Soul" magazine. I appeared on "MARTHA" (her TV show), as well as the major networks, and inspired viewers with the same healthy recipes I had used to lose weight. I spent the next five years growing my magazine, launching another business, appearing on local and national TV and radio programs and flying across the country speaking to large companies and organizations. In 2012, I sold both of my companies ("Women's Running" magazine and my start-up, the Women's Half Marathon series), so I could focus on sharing my knowledge about weight loss to an even broader audience.

The Healthy You Diet is the culmination of my own experiences, as well as those of the thousands of people who have successfully followed the program. (You'll read some of their stories throughout this book.) The Healthy You Diet significantly changed my life, and it can change yours, too.

It's important to showcase your best work in your sample chapters and introduction. Although including an introduction in addition to one or two sample chapters is not mandatory, use your introduction as another opportunity to sell your idea to the publisher. If done correctly, your introduction will do the work for you.

Chapter 10:
Target Audience

Make sure your proposal includes specifics about the target audience for your book. If you have a unique way to reach this market, highlight or restate that advantage in this section of the proposal. I've shared below the target audience details I provided in two of my book proposals— the "Healthy You Diet" and "Winning Nice." Please note: The stats are no longer current, but both write-ups should give you a guideline for what should be included in this section.

Target Audience for the Healthy You Diet

There is an enormous audience for the "Healthy You Diet" cookbook. The target audience encompasses women 25 to 54 who want to eat a cleaner, more wholesome diet. These women also tend to want to lose weight and feel better about themselves, but they haven't yet figured out how.

Studies show that about two-thirds of Americans are overweight or obese and that more than 60% of adults want to lose 20 or more pounds!

According to an ABC News report:

- **108 million** Americans are on diets, and these dieters typically make four to five diet attempts each year!
- Annual revenue of the weight loss industry in America totals **$20 billion!**
- **85% of those** who purchase weight loss products and services are women!

Just on Facebook alone, more than 22 million women ages 21 and older are interested in healthy cooking and weight loss. The *Healthy You! Diet*" cookbook will target these women, as well as women who are simply interested in clean eating as a way to achieve better overall health.

Target Audience for Winning Nice

The core audience for "Winning Nice" is women in business. These women are corporate middle managers and workers, as well as small business owners and entrepreneurs. Dawna's background as both a high-level corporate executive and start-up founder allows her to appeal to and relate to both groups.

According to the Bureau of Labor Statistics, in 2004 there were:

- 44.2 million full-time women workers
- 7.4 million FT women earning more than $50,000 annually
- 11.8 million FT women with some college education
- **13.3 million FT women with a bachelor's degree or higher**

According to the Center for Women's Business Research, in 2004:

- **One in every 11 adult women in the U.S. owned a business**
- 10.6 million privately-held, women-owned businesses existed

- 3.9 million jointly-owned businesses existed

A secondary audience includes women not currently in business, but those either previously in business or who plan to rejoin the workforce in the near future.

In each of the above sections, I also included a brief paragraph about why I was uniquely qualified to reach this particular market. For example, I was regularly being hired to do keynote speaking engagements for women's business groups and nonprofit organizations—some as large as the American Heart Association and Women's Entertainment Television—so I included all those details at the end of the target audience section.

If you have a way to reach your audience, restate it again here. This is not mandatory, but it's a nice bonus for the publisher.

Chapter 11:
Competitive Analysis

Make **sure your proposal** includes a detailed competitive analysis. In 2005, I wrote a book proposal for my business book "Winning Nice: How to Succeed in Business and Life Without Waging War." On the next page, find the competitive analysis section from that book proposal.

You'll note that this section aims to include some of the best-selling books at the time. Include a section introduction, then list four to six books that are similar to yours. State how they're alike as well as why your book stands out or is unique.

You want to show the publisher that a strong market exists for your book and, more importantly, you want to prove why your book will excel in this field of bestsellers.

Use the template on the following page as your starting point.

Competing/Similar Books (From "Winning Nice" Proposal)

"Winning Nice" targets two segments of the business market that have not, to date, been brought together effectively. The first segment encompasses books focusing on the power of positive energy and human relationships. Books in this segment include:

- "How to Win Friends and Influence People" by Dale Carnegie
- "Winning With People" by John C. Maxwell
- "How Full is Your Bucket?" by Tom Rath and Donald O. Clifton

The second segment consists of women-specific business behavior books. These books provide insight into how women can better succeed in the workplace. Books in this segment include:

- "Leading From the Front: No-Excuse Leadership Tactics for Women" by Angie Morgan and Courtney Lynch
- "Nice Girls Don't Get the Corner Office: 101 Unconscious Mistakes Women Make That Sabotage Their Careers" by Lois P. Frankel

- "Play Like a Man, Win Like a Woman: What Men Know About Success that Women Need to Learn" by Gail Evans
- "Pitch Like a Girl: How a Woman Can Be Herself and Still Succeed" by Ronna Lichtenburg
- "The Martha Rules: 10 Essentials for Achieving Success as You Start, Grow or Manage a Business" by Martha Stewart

Based on her experience, Dawna believes a strong need exists for a book addressing issues from the first segment listed above, but given from a woman's perspective.

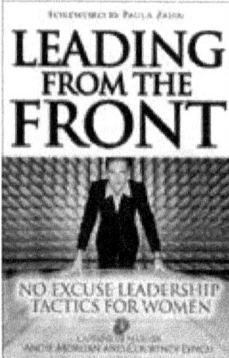

"Leading from the Front: No-Excuse Leadership Tactics for Women"

By: Angie Morgan and Courtney Lynch
Publisher: McGraw-Hill
Pub Date: February 2006

Both former Marine Corps captains, Morgan and Lynch have found that the perseverance, resilience, camaraderie and other leadership skills learned in the military were the secret to their professional success. Much like the Marines, the male-dominated business world requires special navigation techniques for women, and this book reveals 10 key practices that will help transform readers into respected and efficient leaders. For women who want "Marine Corps confidence without the boot camp," this book provides a quick but thorough lesson in effective leadership tactics.

The "Winning Nice" Advantage

While both books effectively build off the careers of the authors, Dawna's girl-next-door appeal and approachability strikes a much more resonate chord with women readers than a book based on military experience.

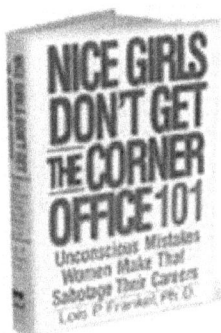

"Nice Girls Don't Get the Corner Office: 101 Unconscious Mistakes Women Make That Sabotage Their Careers"

By: Lois P. Frankel, Ph.D.
Publisher: Warner Business Books
Pub Date: February 2004

For every professional woman who wants to get ahead—but feels she is at an impasse—"Nice Girls Don't Get The Corner Office" comes to the rescue. When overlooked for that special assignment or promotion, many women point the finger outwardly, looking for someone else to blame. Now, Lois P. Frankel presents a different view in this empowering career primer that helps women identify ingrained habits they learned as girls that may be holding them back, such as couching statements in a question, smiling inappropriately, tilting the head while speaking and other mannerisms.

The "Winning Nice" Advantage

The books are similar in that both can be used as an ongoing resource, not just a one-time read. Both books provide detailed "how-to" information in a clear, concise manner. However, "Winning Nice" doesn't base advice off the premise that a woman's childhood behavior sabotages her as an adult. "Winning Nice" tells women (and men) to be themselves and to not fall victim to sexual and business stereotypes.

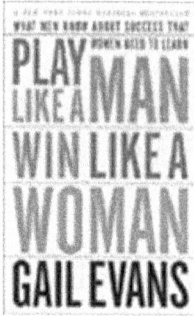

"Play Like a Man, Win Like a Woman: What Men Know About Success that Women Need to Learn"

By: Gail Evans
Publisher: Broadway Books
Pub Date: Sept 2001

Gail Evans reveals the secrets inside this playbook of success and teaches women at all levels of an organization—from assistant to vice president—how to play the game of business to their advantage.

Sharing years of lessons gained from her corporate life, delivered with humor and candor, Gail Evans gives readers practical tools for making the right decisions at work.

Evans is not saying that every woman has to play exactly by men's rules—in fact, not at all. But women do need to know the basic rules so that they can understand the full consequences of every action and how that might impact one's career.

The "Winning Nice" Advantage

"Winning Nice" never assumes that women are less capable of succeeding than men. There is no undercurrent of "men can do this....but women can't." "Winning Nice" is consistently positive and uplifting.

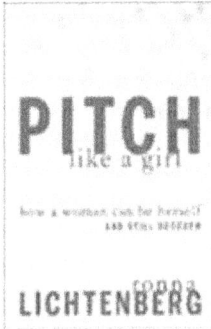

"Pitch Like a Girl: How a Woman Can Be Herself and Still Succeed"

By: Ronna Lichtenburg
Publisher: Rodale Press
Pub Date: January 2005

Shelves lined with business books tell women that the only way to win at work is to behave like a guy. In reality, science shows that the brains of men and women work completely differently.

Starting with recent developments in brain sex research and moving through social stereotypes, Lichtenberg takes a fresh look at how women relate to work and demonstrates how to use one's gifts for desired success.

Lichtenberg, a corporate consultant and contributing editor at "O" magazine, has written a funny and heartfelt how-to manual for women on selling themselves without selling out. The title refers to the proverbial sales pitch and is used throughout as a metaphor for getting what you want. To that end, the author walks readers through the entire process, from visualizing an idea and crafting the pitch to pricing it, sizing up the opponent and presenting. (Source: Library Journal)

The "Winning Nice" Advantage

"Pitch Like a Girl" takes a largely scientific approach to understanding, which behaviors help businesswomen succeed, and it focuses primarily on the concept of the sales pitch. "Winning Nice" is less scientific, more conversational and consequently appeals to a wider audience.

Chapter 12:
Hire a Professional Editor

Make sure your proposal is professionally edited. Too often, writers think their proposal is less important than their book. In truth, your proposal—if trying to get a publishing deal—proves just as important as your book (if not more). Treat it as such, and get your work professionally edited.

Since your proposal will most likely be much shorter than you book, it will also be much less expensive to have edited. All three of my proposals have ranged from 40 to 53 pages in length, whereas my books have ranged from 150 to 300 pages.

If you don't have an editor, you can usually get great recommendations online. If you haven't already, I would suggest joining some author communities or online groups. This is a sure-fire way to get recommendations from other writers.

You can also use a freelance site like upwork.com. Editors range in price from $20 per hour to $100-plus per hour.

Another benefit of getting your proposal professionally edited (besides having a better proposal)? You get to "test drive" an editor who could then become your future book editor. The editor who proofed all of my book proposals went on to edit my books. Not only is this helpful for me as the writer, but the editor also gets a better feel for my work, having been part of the overall process.

Want to make sure you choose the right editor? Ask the editor if he or she will edit only a small section of the proposal (maybe just 10 pages), so you can get a sample of his or her work style and speed. Most professional editors will happily agree to this "test."

Remember, your book proposal represents who you are as a writer and also conveys your book's message and potential for success. Make sure you give it the time and effort it deserves. The better your proposal, the more likely you are to receive a book deal and a larger advance.

Chapter 13:
Exhibits Both Style and Substance

Make sure your proposal has both style AND substance. When I was in graduate school, I wrote a business plan that won a California-wide business plan competition. I don't believe my plan was better than everyone else's. However, I do believe that it had both style and substance, while most of the other competing plans only contained substance. Undoubtedly, substance is by far the most important part of any plan. Yet when you can combine the two—style *and* substance—you have a sure winner!

My business plan was on par with all the other plans when it came to substance, but it also featured color images, a great cover page, graphs, charts, pull quotes and other eye-catching elements. Although I never learned the raw scores or why my submission beat out the competition,

I'm pretty confident that my plan's unique style gave me an extra edge.

Make sure your proposal includes all of the necessary information, is structurally sound and well-written and gets properly proofed; then wow the publisher with your presentation. Use photos and images where needed, or utilize charts and graphs to state your case. Include a cover sample if you have one to show that you've invested time in developing a professional looking book. You can get a cover designed for $50 to $300.

I tend to use a graphic designer who I employed at my previous company. She is fabulous, but charges a little more. I have, however, used online design sites for several other projects, and all provide designers who have book cover experience. Some of these companies include crowd-SPRING, 99designs and Upwork. I've personally used crowdSPRING for many projects over the years and have always received great designs to choose from.

Sites like 99designs and crowdSPRING provide the extra benefit of multiple designers competing for your business. That is, you list your project on the site and interested designers compete by providing their best designs. During the process, you can provide feedback to each designer and they can resubmit based on your ideas. You set the deadline and the award (price). You then select a winner, who provides you with all the design files and receives the award. I have heard good things about 99designs, but I've never personally used the site. I have however used crowd-SPRING for several projects and with great results.

Deadline and Price:

If you use a contest site, you will need to write a project brief—a detailed description of what you are seeking. You will also need to set the timeline or deadline for the project and the award amount, i.e. what you are willing to pay the winner. I usually run the contest for 10 to 14 days and set my award somewhere between $200 and $300, depending on the scope of the project. Note that the higher the award, the more entries you will likely receive—and the more likelihood of having participation from the better designers. But, if you don't have that large of a budget, you can still receive great options for a lower award. Set a budget that works for you.

Chapter 14:
Series Potential

Make sure your proposal states the book's potential for a series, if there is one. If the book really doesn't lend itself to a series, then exclude this section.

Publishers want to know that—if your book succeeds—they can leverage that triumph to gain momentum for future books. A series can be a very attractive opportunity for a publisher. Should your first book be a breakout success, the publisher could potentially reap the rewards of multiple books in a series.

If you can show that you are already considering a series, you build yet another opportunity for book sales—one that the publisher will take into account when deciding to sign you as an author.

Your book's series potential can also garner a larger advance. That is, the publisher will most likely ask for first rights on any subsequent book on the topic. Or, they could give you a deal for multiple books—providing an even larger advance!

I realize this isn't typically something an author thinks about in the early stages of book planning, but it should be. It has become second nature for me to think about the series potential of my books, and it is now even part of my decision making when considering my next idea. A book topic that doesn't lend itself to a series typically doesn't make my "hot list of potential books to write."

Chapter 15:
Testimonials, Praise and Endorsements

If possible, include in your proposal relevant testimonials, praise and endorsements. This is entirely optional, and I've seen proposals done with and without this section. However, if you do have the ability to include this segment, it will strengthen the overall proposal.

Remember, the testimonials must be relevant to the book. For example, if Wolfgang Puck gives a testimonial for a women's business book, it probably won't add any value and may strike the publisher as an odd choice for an endorsement. Yet if you are trying to get a cookbook deal and Wolfgang Puck gives you a glowing review, the publisher likely will be thoroughly impressed and give your proposal a little extra attention.

I was fortunate to have several incredible endorsements for my cookbook, including the two below that proved very relevant in the world of cooking. I'm confident these endorsements helped me get the deal.

As a physician, I know that the hardest step for any patient is the first one. Dawna serves as both a kickstarter and healthy coach. [Her program] CAN change your life.

—Brent Ridge, M.D.

Former Director of Clinical Strategy, Mount Sinai and current star of the Cooking Channel's "The Fabulous Beekman Boys"

I've known Dawna for nearly 10 years. Everything she creates is top-notch, and [her program] proves this once again! Dawna connects with her readers and motivates them to make better food choices. Her mouthwatering recipes prove that eating healthy can be delicious!

—Marcela Valladolid

Chef, cookbook author and a host of the Food Network's "The Kitchen."

I also had numerous endorsements for my first business book, some by lesser-known and some by very well-known individuals. All of them made for a more powerful back cover of the printed book.

I first met Dawna when she was launching her award-winning magazine. As a fellow publisher, I took a special interest in her entrepreneurial aspirations. Dawna stands out as a business leader; her refreshing style not only illustrates the benefits of her philosophy, but it inspires those with goals and dreams to achieve them in a way that leaves the world a better place.

—Steve Forbes

President & CEO and Editor-in-Chief "Forbes Magazine"

The reason Dawna Stone won "The Apprentice: Martha Stewart" is that she is not only smart, good-natured and able to succeed in challenging situations; she is also incredibly NICE. It has been a pleasure knowing Dawna, working with her and advising her. Her book is full of wonderful anecdotes, personal life lessons and advice for others.

—Martha Stewart

As I mentioned previously, I was fortunate to have well-known individuals endorse some of my books. But I didn't have Steve Forbes's or Martha Stewart's endorsements during the proposal phase. Those only came after my manuscript had been completed and I was able to provide them with a copy to review. If you are able to get endorsements from any well-known individuals—even if those endorsements simply discuss you as an individual rather than your book—use them in your proposal.

Getting endorsements isn't easy. It takes a great deal of effort and also requires thick skin, as you will get many more rejections than you will willing takers. But it's time well spent, even if you get only a few that count. And note that it gets easier once you've already gathered your first supporters.

Think of who would make the biggest impression on your specific target market, and approach some of those individuals about providing you with a testimonial. You may need to send them a copy of your completed manuscript, but you will be amazed by how kind and accommodating some people can be.

Most often testimonials and endorsements arrive only after your book has been completed, but sometimes you are able to collect them prior. If you are able, include the most powerful ones you collect in your proposal.

Chapter 16:
Getting the Book Deal vs. DIY

Even though you are now equipped with the steps required to create a great book proposal, getting a book deal remains a difficult undertaking. Just remember: 12 publishers rejected J.K. Rowling before she received a book deal for her "Harry Potter" series. Margaret Mitchell received 38 rejection letters for "Gone with the Wind" before getting a publishing deal. And according to Jack Canfield, his famous "Chicken Soup for the Soul" was rejected a grand total of 144 times!

You may go through many rejections before you find a publisher who wants to work with you. If you really want a traditionally-published book and you truly believe an audience exists for your book, don't give up. Listen to the feedback you receive, make changes if necessary, and find a publisher who believes in your talent as much as you do. But remember, you have options. You can continue to search for a publisher or you can take matters into your own hands and self-publish your work.

I have been fortunate to have both traditionally-published and self-published books, and I can honestly say that one way is not better than the other. In fact, each option has its own set of pros and cons. As the author, you just need to decide what works best for you and your end goal.

Sometimes that decision is made for you. My second book was only self-published because I couldn't get a publisher to give me a deal. It was turned down again and again. So instead of shelving the idea or spending any more time trying to get a publisher, I decided to try my hand at self-publishing. I was passionate about the book, and I believed there was an audience for it, so I moved forward on my own. My self-published book did so well that the same publishers who initially rejected my idea now expressed major interest in the book. That self-published book landed me a six-figure book deal!

I know this book covers writing the best book proposal possible to earn yourself a lucrative book deal, but I still believe self-publishing can be a great option for most first-time authors. It's simple, it's quick, and it gives you complete control over your product. Let's look at the pros and cons of self-publishing:

Pros:

- Uncomplicated
- Short lead time
- Full ownership/copyright of your work
- Complete control of your schedule
- You call all the shots
- Higher profits from book sales
- Inexpensive to publish with today's tools

Cons:

- No advance
- Need to hire your own editor
- Need to design and format your own book cover and interior pages
- No outside marketing support
- Typically no bookstore sales

Now that you know the pros and cons of self-publishing, let's look at the pros and cons of traditional publishing, too.

Pros:

- Possible advance
- Marketing support
- Graphic/design support
- Bookstore distribution

Cons:

- Long lead time (can take more than a year to publish your book)
- No or little control over your book design
- Publisher owning the copyright
- Difficulty in getting accepted by a publisher
- Often the necessity to write a book proposal
- Often the necessity for an agent to get you in the door/land a deal
- Only receiving a small portion of sales—often as little as $1 per book

If you picked up this book, you are most likely trying to get a book deal; I'm confident that these proposal writing tips will help. However, if you don't initially land a deal, it doesn't mean you won't get one in the future. If you want to try your hand at self-publishing, remember that your self-published book can eventually turn into a very lucrative traditional book deal.

If you're interested in learning more about the self-publishing process, check out my work "Book Accelerator: How to Write a Bestseller in 16 Weeks: Boost Your Business, Increase Your Income and Get Noticed." The book will take you step by step through the process of writing and self-publishing your book. If you want some extra hand-holding along the way, you might also choose to join my online "Book Accelerator" course. You can learn more about *Book Accelerator* and the Book Accelerator online course at: www.BookAccelerator.com

The Book Accelerator course, will take you in stages through the book writing, self-publishing and marketing processes. The seven modules and more than 30 lessons will help you:

- Perfect your vision and concept

- Determine your audience

- Find your voice

- Convey the problem and solution in a way that intrigues your reader

- Develop a book structure that works

- Write a killer introduction

- Capture the reader's attention

- Use Mind Mapping and Diamond Mapping™ to build your detailed outline
- Build successful writing habits
- Make the editing process a smooth one
- Develop a title that sells
- Create a cover that captivates!
- Build buzz for your launch
- Market your book
- Monetize your book
- Hit the bestseller list!

Each module has been designed to take you through the Book Accelerator methodology. Each lesson provides clear and concise information to help you not only keep the momentum going, but also to eliminate the stress of writing and make the process fun.

Finding a traditional book publisher can take a long time no matter how strong your proposal. Should you decide to self-publish, following the Book Accelerator methodology can help.

The Book Accelerator methodology is a proven process to get you from the idea stage to finished book in less than 16 weeks. If you're motivated to write your book, the Book Accelerator online course will provide you with the additional accountability you need to push past time constraints and to make your writing a priority. Don't let anything hold you back from your dream of becoming an author. It's time to write a book that will boost your business or career, increase your income and get you noticed! You can learn more and see the course curriculum at www.BookAccelerator.com

Whether you self-publish your book or use my blueprint to write a book proposal that sells, don't waste another moment. Get started today!

Please share your successes with me. I'd love to hear about your proposal writing experiences, the feedback you receive along the way and the books you publish! Stay connected by emailing me at Dawna@BookAccelerator.com

To my valued readers,

Thank you for taking time to read *How to Write a Book Proposal That Sells!* I hope you were able to take away some valuable information that will help you write your proposal.

As an author or future author you probably know how important it is to get positive reviews for your book. I would be so thankful it if you could take a minute and provide an honest review for this book. **Thank you so much!**

To your author success!

Dawna Stone